3-00

**LAKE FOREST
CHILDREN'S LIBRARY**

360 E. DEERPATH

LAKE FOREST, IL 60045

234-0648

DEMCO

Cities through Time

Daily Life in
Ancient and Modern

by *Dawn Kotapish*

illustrations by Ray Webb

RP

Runestone Press/Minneapolis
A Division of Lerner Publishing Group

The *Cities through Time* series is produced by Runestone Press, a division of Lerner Publishing Group, in cooperation with Greenleaf Publishing, Inc., Geneva, Illinois.

Text design by Melanie Lawson, Jean DeVaty, and Rebecca JonMichaels. Cover design by Michael Tacheny.

Runestone Press
A Division of Lerner Publishing Group
241 First Avenue North
Minneapolis, Minnesota 55401 U.S.A.

Website address: www.lernerbooks.com

Library of Congress Cataloging-in-Publication Data

Kotapish, Dawn.
     Daily life in ancient and modern Baghdad/by Dawn Kotapish; illustrated by Ray Webb.
        p.   cm. — (Cities through time)
     Includes index.
     Summary: A historical exploration of events and daily life in Baghdad in both ancient and modern times.
        ISBN 0-8225-3219-0 (lib. bdg. : alk. paper)
        1. Baghdad (Iraq)—Social life and customs—Juvenile literature.
     [Baghdad (Iraq)]   I. Webb, Ray, ill.   II. Title.   III. Series.
     DS79.9.K68   2000
     956.7'47—dc21   98-53960

Manufactured in the United States of America
1 2 3 4 5 6 – JR – 05 04 03 02 01 00

Contents

Introduction

Modern-day Baghdad is the capital of Iraq, a Middle Eastern nation bordering Iran, Kuwait, Saudi Arabia, Jordan, Syria, and Turkey. The Republic of Iraq was founded in 1932, but Baghdad has been a major city since it was built in A.D. 762 as the capital of the Islamic Empire.

Baghdad spreads over both banks of the Tigris River, about 30 miles from the Euphrates River. The land between the rivers—historically known as Mesopotamia—has soil good for farming, unlike most of the arid Middle East. Powerful and important cities have flourished in the area for thousands of years.

In 3500 B.C., Sumer flourished in the southern part of present-day Iraq, where the Tigris and Euphrates join. Sumerians built irrigation canals to improve the land for farming. They constructed towering temples known as ziggurats. They also developed a complex system of government and the earliest known written language.

Babylon—another important ancient city—dominated the region from 2300 B.C. until 1600 B.C. The Babylonians expanded and improved the Sumerian irrigation system. Nineveh, near the modern-day Iraqi city of Mosul, was the capital of the Assyrian Empire, which reigned from 900 B.C. until 600 B.C. The Persian Empire was ruled from Ctesiphon, just 20 miles south of Baghdad, until A.D. 637.

When the Islamic Empire's fortunes eventually declined, so did Baghdad's. But in the twentieth century, the discovery of oil greatly improved the city's prospects. In 1932 Baghdad became the thriving capital of the independent nation of Iraq. In recent years, Iraq has incurred significant damage during several wars. But Baghdad has not lost its place as a major metropolis of the Middle East.

Tigris River

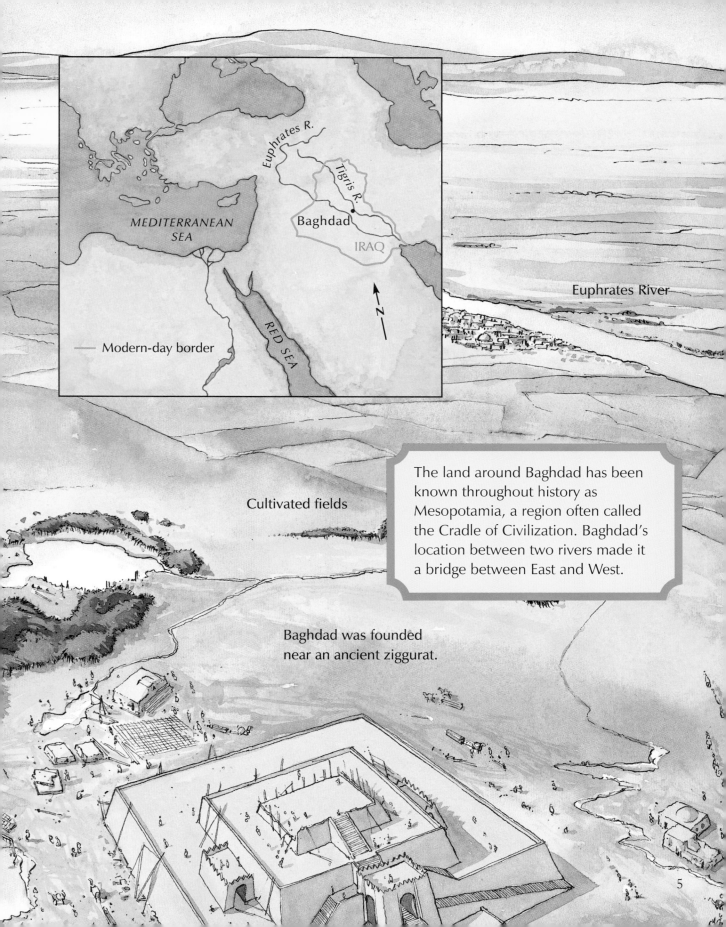

MEDITERRANEAN SEA

Euphrates R.

Tigris R.

Baghdad

IRAQ

N

RED SEA

— Modern-day border

Euphrates River

Cultivated fields

The land around Baghdad has been known throughout history as Mesopotamia, a region often called the Cradle of Civilization. Baghdad's location between two rivers made it a bridge between East and West.

Baghdad was founded near an ancient ziggurat.

The Islamic Empire

In the A.D. 600s, nomadic peoples from the Arabian Peninsula became Muslims, or followers of the Islamic religion. According to Islam, a holy man named Muhammad received messages from Allah, the one true God. Muhammad recorded these revelations in a holy book, the Koran. The belief system united many of the people of the Arabian Peninsula. Within a hundred years of Islam's beginning, Muslims forged an empire that dominated Persia, northern Egypt, and the Arabian Peninsula. By the eighth century, the empire controlled North Africa, Spain, and land extending into China and India.

As the empire grew, various clans and dynasties (ruling families) claimed the throne. In 750 the Abbasid dynasty gained control of the empire. It took its name from Abbas, the prophet Muhammad's paternal uncle and an Abbasid ancestor.

The prophet Muhammad (veiled because Islam forbids that his face be depicted) receives messages from an angel (*opposite*). Early Baghdad (*above*) spreads serenely along the banks of the Tigris.

This is an excellent place for a military camp. Here is the Tigris to keep us in touch with lands as far as China and bring us all that the seas yield. It will also give us the food products of Mesopotamia, Armenia, and their adjacent territories. And there is the Euphrates to carry for us all that Syria, Rakka, and their adjacent territories have to offer.
—al-Mansur

In 762 the second Abbasid caliph (ruler), al-Mansur, moved the empire's capital from Damascus (located in what would become Syria) to a tiny Persian village named Baghdad. For many reasons, the village was the perfect site for the Islamic Empire's new capital. Enemies would have to cross either the Tigris River or the Euphrates River to attack.

The rivers made the fields around the city into very fertile farmland. They also allowed commerce and trade to flourish. Also, Baghdad's location wasn't plagued with mosquitoes, as was most of Iraq. Within decades Baghdad had become an intellectual capital as well as the seat of the Abbasid caliphate.

EARLY BAGHDAD

I have visited the greatest cities…but I have never seen a city raised to greater heights and more perfectly round, with wider gates, or with such imposing walls.
—author al-Jahiz, writing of Baghdad

Outer wall

City wall

Inner wall

Caliph's palace and mosque

Al-Mansur Founds Baghdad

Al-Mansur laid the first brick of his city in A.D. 762. Four years later, a hundred thousand artisans, architects, carpenters, and other laborers completed the spectacular new capital. The nearest source of stone was 80 miles away, so builders made clay bricks, some weighing as much as 200 pounds.

Baghdad became known across the empire as the Round City because of the walls that encircled it. A smooth outer wall, topped with many watchtowers, protected mud-brick houses, mosques (Islamic houses of worship), and suqs (marketplaces). A second wall ringed the city's center. Nearly 100 feet tall, this massive wall was 145 feet thick at its base and 40 feet thick at the top. The iron gates were so heavy that several strong guards had to open and close them.

A third inner wall with an enormous golden gate protected the palace where the caliph lived with his wives, children, slaves, and bodyguards. Here the caliph could feel safe from attacks by rivals and enemies. The ornate palace boasted a 130-foot-high green dome and countless smaller ones. Legend says that the dome was topped with a statue of a horseman that would turn to point at an approaching enemy. Homes for the caliph's adult children and offices for secretaries and government aides also were housed in the city's center. So were huge, opulent halls where caliphs entertained ambassadors, poets, philosophers, and historians. The palace mosque had a gleaming teakwood roof painted the color of lapis lazuli, a bright blue gemstone.

Like a great wheel, Baghdad spread out from its hub (*left*), where the caliph's palace and mosque were located.

Life in the Round City

So many people flocked to Baghdad that the space between the two outer walls became crowded. Marketplaces were moved south of the city, and new palaces were built across the river. Soon suburbs bursting with houses, mosques, shops, bathhouses, and suqs spread across the banks of the Tigris. Within a few decades, Baghdad blossomed into a center of international trade, political might, and cultural influence. Only a hundred years after its founding, the city's population hovered at one million people.

A small group of very wealthy royalty and landowners lived in great luxury. But most people worked hard seven days a week. Some men were shopkeepers, merchants, artisans, craftsmen, surgeons, or healers. Other men entertained the upper class as fortune-tellers, astrologists, dream interpreters, hypnotists, glass-chewers, and sword-swallowers. Scholars, mathematicians, and poets from across the Islamic Empire—especially from Persia—flocked to Baghdad looking for patronage (support from a rich person) and to take part in the famous intellectual life of the city.

Men and women had separate quarters. Most people lived in low, mud-brick houses. Women hid their faces behind

> *Let not the longing of your soul for family and home prevent your enjoying an easy life in comfort; in every country where you choose to dwell, you will find a family and [friendly] neighbors in place of those you left behind.*
> —Advice of the ninth-century poet Muslim ibn al-Walid al-Ansari

veils. They rarely associated with men outside their family. Among the working class, women ran households, spun thread, wove cloth, and cared for children. In the kitchen, they crushed homegrown wheat and cooked meals, mixing grain with vegetables such as eggplant and cabbage. Some enterprising women ran home businesses, wove rugs in small workshops, or made other handicrafts to sell to supplement the family income. Young girls fetched fuel—usually wood or animal dung—for the cooking fire. The girls shaped the dung into patties that they hung on outdoor walls to dry in the sun. Boys helped their fathers at work or went to school.

As depicted in this nineteenth-century image, medieval Baghdad's canals and bridges were lively avenues of traffic and commerce.

A typical suq opened in the early morning. Merchants sold everything from basic foodstuffs like rice to luxury goods such as gold, silk, and perfume.

We know that hither came all the products of the world in constant stream. Spices of all kinds, aloes and sandalwood for fumigation, teak for shipbuilding, ebony for artistic work, jewels, metals, dyes, and minerals of all kinds...
—A Baghdad merchant

Suqs and Caravans

Baghdad's merchants traveled across Asia and into Europe and Africa. Many traveled in long caravans of camels. Even carrying trade goods and passengers, camels could tolerate the hot days and cold nights of Baghdad's surrounding deserts. By traveling in a group, merchants gained protection from thieves, thirst, and starvation. Journeys could last for months. A caravan usually started before sunrise and traveled about three miles an hour for up to twelve hours a day.

Medieval woodcut of a caravan in transit

Other merchants sailed the seas. Trade ships, pleasure vessels, warships, and rafts made of inflated sheepskins sailed from the Persian Gulf up the rivers to the city's shipping docks.

Over land and by sea, merchants traveled to and from China bringing silk, porcelain, musk, paper, and ink. From India came spices, minerals, and dyes. Central Asia was the source of fabrics and gemstones. From Scandinavia and Russia, merchants brought honey, wax, furs, falcons, armor, and white slaves. African merchants traded gold, ivory, ebony, and black slaves.

Merchants brought their goods to Baghdad's crowded, noisy suqs. Small, windowless stores opened onto narrow, crowded streets full of busy traders and shoppers. The suqs were divided up into areas that sold specific items. Merchants sold rice, grain, linen, silks, pearls, weapons, perfumes, dates, fruits and vegetables, glass, and mirrors. Shoppers could be sure of a good bargain with competitors sitting side by side. Merchants often offered their customers stools upon which to sit while examining goods and bargaining. All of this international trade and flow of money encouraged a popular new profession—banking.

An Empire's Religion

The Islamic empire was united by religion. As the seat of the caliphate, Baghdad was an important center of Islam. The Abbasid caliphs were descendants of Muhammad's uncle Abbas. The caliph was called the Shadow of God on Earth. During special religious celebrations, he put on a mantle that the prophet Muhammad was believed to have worn. The caliph employed religious leaders called mullahs to aid and advise him.

The Muslim people of Baghdad observed the Five Pillars of Islam—faith, prayer, giving to the poor, fasting, and pilgrimage to the holy city of Mecca (in what would become Saudi Arabia). Every day Muslim men went to one of Baghdad's mosques. Pious followers prayed five times a day, rising at dawn for the first prayer. During the holy month called Ramadan, Muslims followed strict rules for fasting and prayer.

At the end of Ramadan, wealthy citizens held feasts for the poor. They piled dishes with delicacies, such as chicken and veal sautéed with eggplant and simmered in pomegranate juice and cardamom. Lamb was stuffed with fruit, nuts, and onions. People ate with the fingers of their right hands. One could guarantee the cleanliness of one's fingers but not of someone else's utensils.

Many villagers living near Baghdad were *dhimmis* (non-Muslims including Christians, Jews, and Zoroastrians). Caliphs allowed dhimmis to practice their own religions. But dhimmis also had to pay a special tax. Some caliphs imposed other rules on the dhimmis. In A.D. 850, Caliph al-Mutawakkil made Jews and Christians wear yellow coats and attach balls to the saddles of their mules or donkeys. In addition, Muslim jurors couldn't accept a non-Muslim's word over that of a Muslim. Despite the restrictions, many dhimmis prospered. By the late ninth century, some Christians had become viziers (the caliph's right-hand men), and Jews had held high government offices. By 1170 Baghdad boasted 10 rabbinical schools and 23 synagogues.

Among the cities of the world, Baghdad stands out as the professor of the community of Islam.
    —A foreign dignitary upon returning home from a visit to ninth-century Baghdad

Young People

Little boys and girls lived with their mothers in the women's section of a Baghdad home. But at age seven, a boy left his mother, sisters, aunts, and grandmother for the men's part of the household. The boy's father began to teach him the manners expected of a man in Baghdad. Boys learned to be frugal in eating, not to talk too much, to avoid spitting in public, and not to speak badly of anyone.

Many boys were enrolled in Islamic schools where they learned how to read, write, and do arithmetic. Early Baghdad boasted about 30 schools, each affiliated with a mosque. Education centered around memorizing passages of the Koran and other poetry.

Loom

Boys from wealthy or royal families enjoyed the instruction of private tutors. Girls might receive some basic religious instruction. Instead of going to school, most girls helped their mothers with the many tasks of running a household. They learned to make jam and sauces, bake bread, and practice hospitality by entertaining guests.

Young people played many games. Some children had stone-throwing contests. Most liked to play knucklebones, a game that involved tossing in the air small, six-sided bones from sheep legs. Chess was popular, too. And the waters of canals and the Euphrates and Tigris Rivers offered boys opportunities for swimming, fishing, and sailing toy boats.

Koran

Tutor

Marriage and Family

Marriage was seen as a duty to family, society, and God in early Baghdad. Women married between the ages of 12 and 20. Men typically married around the age of 20. Families arranged the marriages usually without the bride's consent. The bride's mother or aunt often made the initial arrangements with the prospective groom's mother. The groom or his father then approached the bride's father. The two families decided if their wealth and social status made a good match. Finally they signed a contract affirming the girl's age and the dowry.

The dowry was a sum of money, jewelry, and gifts that the groom's family paid to the bride's family, who then bestowed the gifts upon the young bride. The size of the dowry depended on the wealth of the family and the beauty and youth of the bride. After marriage, the bride went to live with her husband's family. In the event of a divorce, the bride was often allowed to keep her dowry.

Men usually married one woman. But some claimed their right under Islam to have up to four wives who had to be treated equally. Each wife and her children needed their own slaves and their own living, sleeping, and cooking quarters.

Children were viewed as a great blessing among Baghdad families. Baby boys were especially celebrated and often welcomed by a week of feasting. Family members stepped up to whisper into the newborn's ear the sacred Islamic oath: "There is no God but Allah, and Muhammad is his prophet." On the fortieth day after the child's birth, parents invited their friends and neighbors for a feast to officially welcome the child into the community.

A baby was dressed in a tiny shirt and firmly swaddled (tightly wrapped) in cloth. Swaddling restricted the baby's movement and kept the child secure so that he or she could more easily be transported on the back of a camel, hung on a tree branch while the mother worked, or laid next to a fire for warmth.

Marriage was seen as the most important milestone in the life of a young person. Divorce was possible. To divorce his wife, a husband had to repeat the words "I divorce you" three times in the presence of witnesses. A wife had no such rights. If she succeeded in getting a divorce, she risked forfeiting the return of her dowry.

19

Hunting, Games, and Baths

Hunting, trapping, and falconry were favorite pastimes among Baghdad's residents. Desert nomads living on Baghdad's outskirts hunted with falcons. The falcon, a superior hunter, could comb great distances by air and swoop down on smaller birds. Bird meat provided a healthy supplement and a welcome variation to the local diet.

Mounted on a horse with a large falcon perched on his arm, a falconer needed great skill to control the bird. The falconer had to train the bird every day, or else it would return to the wild. After the falcon caught its game, the falconer quickly followed. He slit the captured animal's throat, according to Islamic custom. The falcon received food as a reward.

Within the city, people enjoyed games. Chess was so popular that caliphs invited champion chess players—free people and slaves alike—to matches at the palace. People in Baghdad also liked such Persian games as backgammon.

Public bathhouses were major centers of recreation and social life. The baths were open to all but slaves. Women could visit bathhouses on certain days.

Elaborate mosaic floors and marble walls made bathhouses spectacular. Attendants poured hot and cold water over bathers, who could not only wash but also relax in a pool or in a warm room. People socialized in outer rooms, where refreshments were served. Bathers who could afford it ate delicious meals of soup, bread, fattened chicken, and wine flavored with Syrian apples.

21

The Slave Trade

Slaves were common in Baghdad, and not just as servants. Legions of warrior slaves—called Mamluks—protected the caliph. In Central Asia, the caliph's agents purchased young men to train as warriors and brought them to Baghdad. The Mamluks made up an entire army, which eventually grew mightier than the caliphate itself.

Most slaves were captured in wars or purchased from slave traders. They included people of Turkish, African, Armenian, Greek, and Slavic origin. It was illegal to enslave a Muslim, although a slave would not be set free for converting to Islam.

Slaves did not always live their entire lives in captivity. Some owners set their slaves free or let them earn money to buy their freedom. People who had been captured in wars could be ransomed by relatives in their home country.

Some slaves lived miserable lives draining marshes and doing other difficult work. Other slaves worked in households, on small farms, and in businesses. And many performers—singers, dancers, and poets—were slaves who had been trained in their skills. Although some slave owners were cruel, many others obeyed the prophet Muhammad, who told his followers to treat their slaves well. A man named al-Yaqubi was purchased in Baghdad by a traveling merchant, who educated al-Yaqubi and eventually freed him. In time al-Yaqubi became one of the Islamic Empire's greatest geographers.

Free men sometimes took female slaves as wives. The children of these women were considered free. Many caliphs were born of slave mothers. (Children with two slave parents remained slaves however.) An orphan could be adopted as a slave. For instance, an orphaned boy might tend sheep for a village family. In exchange, the family would give the orphan food, shelter, basic clothing, and a few sheep of his own each year.

A typical Baghdad slave market, seen in this medieval illustration, sold people of all nationalities.

And your slaves! See that ye feed them with such food as ye eat yourselves, and clothe them with the like clothing as ye wear yourselves.

—The prophet Muhammad

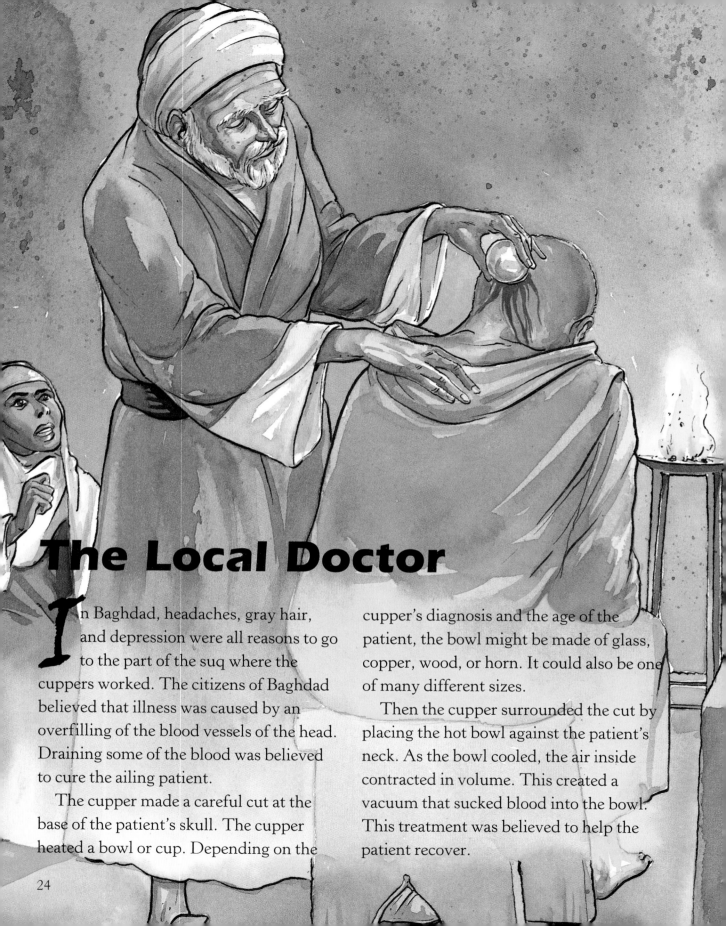

The Local Doctor

In Baghdad, headaches, gray hair, and depression were all reasons to go to the part of the suq where the cuppers worked. The citizens of Baghdad believed that illness was caused by an overfilling of the blood vessels of the head. Draining some of the blood was believed to cure the ailing patient.

The cupper made a careful cut at the base of the patient's skull. The cupper heated a bowl or cup. Depending on the cupper's diagnosis and the age of the patient, the bowl might be made of glass, copper, wood, or horn. It could also be one of many different sizes.

Then the cupper surrounded the cut by placing the hot bowl against the patient's neck. As the bowl cooled, the air inside contracted in volume. This created a vacuum that sucked blood into the bowl. This treatment was believed to help the patient recover.

Cupping was an important part of everyday life. A royal festival called the Feast of the Cupping was held near the caliph's birthday every year. Guests presented the caliph with gifts to encourage his good health.

Baghdad's doctors worked hard to help improve people's lives. One physician, Hunayn ibn Ishaq al-Ibadi, was praised for his ethics when he was thrown into prison for refusing to concoct a poison for an enemy of Caliph al-Mutawakkil. When the caliph asked him to relent, the imprisoned doctor refused. He said, "My religion decrees that we should do good even to our enemies, how much more to our friends. And my profession is instituted for the benefit of humanity."

25

Village Life

An ingenious system of canals gave Baghdad's residents a good supply of fresh, clean water. The caliphs of Baghdad reopened the ancient Babylonian canals. This intricate system that carried water from the Tigris and the Euphrates Rivers to the fields had long been neglected. When repaired, water from the rivers flowed through vaulted tunnels running underground to farmers' fields and to neighborhood wells. Other canals formed small rivers, some deep and wide enough for ships to pass through.

The canals irrigated the land near Baghdad, making it good for farming. In fact, the irrigation system helped the city grow enough grain to feed its enormous

population as well as to export food to other parts of the world.

Rich landowners—many of whom lived in the city—owned much of the country-side surrounding Baghdad. They rented the land to farmers. Most farmers lived in villages and raised crops of grains and cotton. Many of these farmers were Persians whose ancestors had worked the land before the Islamic Empire absorbed the region. Although they lived on the outskirts of the city, they were considered residents of Baghdad. Most farm families lived in one-room homes, often sharing their quarters with their livestock. Men and women worked side by side in the fields all day long and traveled to the city's suqs to trade their crops and crafts.

I mention Baghdad first of all because it is the heart of Iraq, and, with no equal on earth either in the Orient or the Occident, it is the most extensive city in area, in importance, in prosperity, in abundance of water, and in healthful climate.... People emigrate to it from all countries, both near and far, and everywhere there are men who have preferred it to their own country.

—al-Yaqubi, geographer and former slave, writing 150 years after Baghdad's founding

I have never entered a town which I did not consider just another place in a journey except Baghdad, for when I entered it I considered it my home.
　　—The scholar al-Shafi'i of Gaza

The House of Wisdom

When Muslim forces defeated a Chinese army in 751, Chinese prisoners taught their captors how to make paper. By 794 Baghdad had its first paper mill. Schools, bookshops, and libraries soon sprang up all over the Muslim world. By the tenth century, Baghdad's suqs boasted as many as a hundred bookshops. Each book had to be hand copied—printing presses had not yet been invented.

Baghdad was home to one of Islam's greatest libraries—the House of Wisdom, established in 830 by Caliph al-Ma'mun. Scholars from across the Middle East flocked to the caliph's court and to the House of Wisdom. Persian and Indian teachings were translated into Arabic. Baghdad's scholars also translated Greek treatises on mathematics, astronomy, medicine, and philosophy. And Baghdad's scholars made their own contributions. The scientist al-Khwarizmi, who flourished in Caliph al-Ma'mun's court, is considered the father of astronomy.

But not all the books in Baghdad were for learning. People used to listen to wonderful stories populated with princes, princesses, thieves, wizards, and genies. Many of the stories had roots in ancient Indian and Persian tales. One of Baghdad's most famous story collections, *One Thousand and One Nights,* was translated into Arabic in the tenth century. Storytellers in Baghdad and across the Islamic Empire added new details. Some of the well-known stories include "Aladdin and the Magic Lamp," "Ali Baba and the Forty Thieves," and "The Adventures of Sinbad the Sailor." Other tales were based on the exploits of members of the royal Abbasid family.

The High Life

Only 50 years after it was founded, Baghdad entered the period of its greatest prosperity, under Caliph Harun al-Rashid. According to legend, al-Rashid ascended the throne after his bloodthirsty brother, Caliph Musa, tried to poison his own mother. When the plot failed, Musa's mother bribed some slave girls to smother Musa with pillows as he slept. Al-Rashid, already a military hero, then took the throne.

As the capital of the enormous Islamic Empire, Baghdad's royal court attracted foreign dignitaries from across Europe, Africa, and Asia. Poets, scholars, musicians, singers, dancers, and jesters flocked to Baghdad to entertain the caliph and to live in what was called the richest city on earth. Zubaydah, al-Rashid's wife, decorated her shoes with gemstones. She refused to drink from any cup not made of gold and silver and ornamented with precious stones. Thousands of richly woven carpets adorned the palaces, which had zoos, gardens, and splendid chambers.

But al-Rashid was not the only extravagant caliph. The evening wedding of Caliph al-Ma'mun to his 18-year-old bride, Buran, in 825 was called one of the most extravagant events of the age. Thousands of burning candles illuminated the wedding couple seated upon a mat made of gold and sapphires. A thousand pearls were showered upon their heads. Wedding guests received gifts of land, slaves, gold, and silver.

But not everything about being rich was wonderful. Many women were hardly ever allowed to go outside—not even with their husbands. In fact, some women were kept inside from their marriages until their deaths. At times this caused poor health because they rarely saw the sun.

> A story is told of the day when Caliph al-Amin's bodyguard delivered a caged lion to his door. At al-Amin's order, the guard let it loose. It was a particularly savage lion, and the servant fled in fear. Al-Amin sat watching the lion while he finished his drink. Suddenly, the lion crouched and sprang. Al-Amin responded by grabbing a cushion, holding it out in front of him, and plunging his dagger into the lion, killing it.
> —Arab tale

In this nineteenth-century painting (*right*), Harun al-Rashid receives European dignitaries at court.

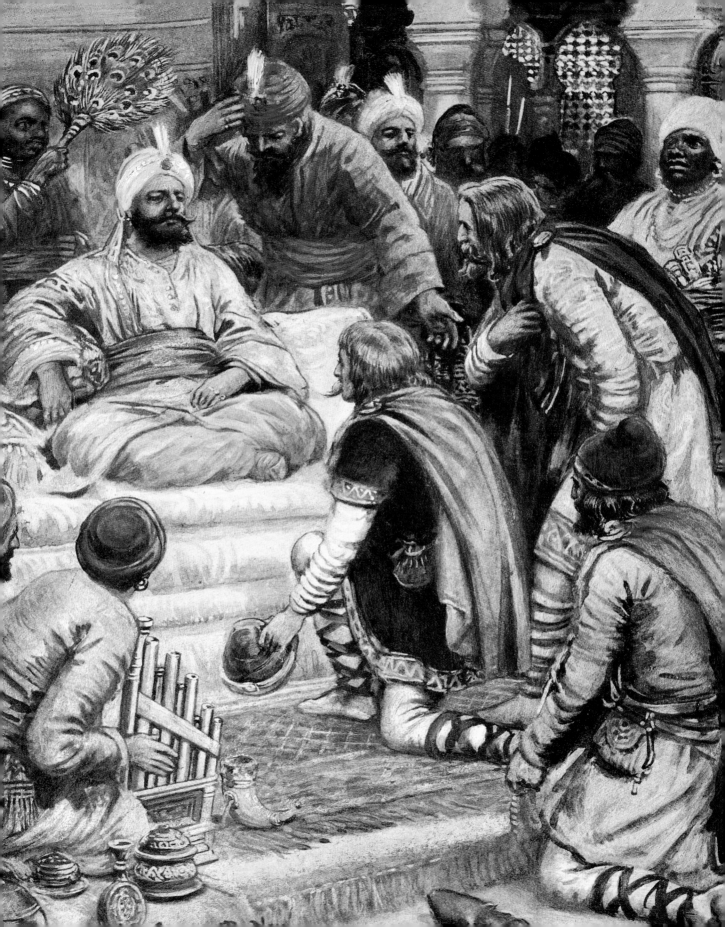

Civil War Erupts

Although the caliphs were rich, trouble was on its way. At its height, the Islamic Empire stretched across all of North Africa into Spain and Asia. Islam united the different cultures, lifestyles, and histories of this huge empire into one powerful entity. But a split between two Muslim factions—Sunni and Shia—weakened the unity of the far-flung empire. Local leaders became more powerful than distant caliphs. Spain broke away in 756, Morocco in 788, and Tunisia in 800. Egypt left the empire in 868.

As the capital of the Islamic Empire, Baghdad's fortunes were tied to the empire's. When Caliph Harun al-Rashid died in 806, his son al-Amin became caliph. But Amin's brother al-Ma'mun, with full Persian support, fought Amin for the throne. In the resulting civil war, people of Persian origin sided with al-Amin. Those of Arab origin sided with al-Ma'mun.

Al-Ma'mun soon had Baghdad under siege. Food became scarce. Rich people were able to bribe enemy soldiers to bring them food, but the poor were starving. Roving bands of hungry people and criminals robbed shops and homes. Well-off people hired teams of bodyguards. In 813 al-Ma'mun's forces defeated al-Amin and his army, captured Baghdad, and ended the war. Large parts of the city had been destroyed in the fighting. And tensions between Persian and Arab people had become a fact of life.

Most of the people who lived in the city of Baghdad were Arabs, but Persian people lived in the nearby countryside.

Persian customs had influenced many aspects of life. Most people in Baghdad wore Persian-style clothes. Persian household items—including mattresses, cushions, ovens, and frying pans—were standard in most homes. Meals were served on tables, a novelty to Arabs used to eating as they sat cross-legged on the floor. Over time, many Persian and Arab people had married. Even so, the two groups grew more wary of each other.

Al-Ma'mun won the civil war, but the role of caliph became less powerful as Mamluk armies grew in power and influence. In the next centuries, Baghdad would be further weakened by a series of invasions.

The civil war that swept the Islamic Empire in the ninth century was bloody and divisive (*left*). Mamluk warriors (*right*) took power from the caliphs.

Fires and Floods

The eleventh and twelfth centuries were a period of decline for Baghdad. The caliphs lost more power as the Mamluk armies gained control of the empire. Rule of the city passed from one faction to the next, with the caliphs presiding as figureheads.

Baghdad suffered from natural disasters that joined the political turmoil to erode the city's power. From its founding, Baghdad had suffered from damage caused by strong winds, torrential rains, hail, drought, and locusts.

In 1092 a fire broke out that consumed much of the suq, including the money-changers' markets, the goldsmiths' section, and the stalls where dried fruit and fragrant flowers were sold. This was followed by more fires. An earthquake in 1117 destroyed many neighborhoods on the city's west bank. Looters ransacked damaged buildings across the city.

In 1146 Caliph al-Muqtafi had just arrived at his palace when it caught fire. Amazingly, no one died. The caliph was so grateful for this that he gave money to the poor and freed many prisoners.

Because of the political infighting during this period, the canals that brought water from the Tigris and Euphrates Rivers to the farmers' fields were neglected. This meant that less food could be grown in the fields, and it made the area more vulnerable to floods. In 1174 one of the worst natural disasters in the city's history struck. A severe rainstorm caused the Tigris River to overflow its banks. Water reached a level 18 inches higher than any recorded since the city's founding. Although residents scrambled to fill holes in the dikes, the rain kept falling and soon the dikes burst. Canals overflowed, and the city streets flooded, drowning many people. Mud-brick homes dissolved or collapsed, destroying large parts of the city. The Adud al-Daula Hospital was so flooded that boats carrying the patients just floated in through the windows.

Many Baghdad residents drowned when the terrible floods of the twelfth century inundated the city.

The Mongols Sack the City

In 1258 a new threat emerged when the Mongols (a people from eastern Asia) approached Baghdad. The invasion was led by Hülegü Khan, the grandson of Mongol leader Genghis Khan. Fierce Mongol warriors killed al-Mustasim, the last caliph of Baghdad, and murdered Baghdad's scholars, religious leaders, and writers, along with thousands of other residents. They used the skulls of the dead to build gruesome pyramids.

Hülegü also ordered that Baghdad's remaining canals and dikes be destroyed. He burned books and destroyed artwork. With the irrigation system destroyed, Baghdad's farmers could produce little food. The city became a part of the vast Mongol Empire, which stretched across much of Asia and was ruled from Tabriz, in what would become Iran.

Another wave of Mongol invaders, led by Tamerlane, swept across Asia to Baghdad in 1401. Baghdad's residents were determined to resist. They closed the city's gates and set up soldiers to patrol the walls. The summer heat was so intense it was said that birds fell from the sky. But Tamerlane commanded his troops to set siege to the city.

For 40 days, Tamerlane and his soldiers waited in the baking heat for a chance to invade. Finally the city's watchmen decided to go indoors to cool off. They arranged their helmets just above the parapets, hoping to trick the Mongol army into thinking soldiers were still on guard. But Tamerlane's men discovered the trick, climbed the walls, and stormed the city, killing thousands.

Despite his ferocity, Tamerlane was a patron of the arts. During the bloodbath, he gathered the city's artists, poets, and scholars. He gave them horses and commanded them to flee.

The invasion of Baghdad by Tamerlane *(facing page)* left the city in ruins. Every building except for mosques, schools, and hospitals had been destroyed.

You ask me about the sack of Baghdad. It was so horrible there are no words to describe it. I wish I'd died earlier and not seen how the fools destroyed these treasures of knowledge and learning. I thought I understood the world, but this holocaust is so strange and pointless that I'm struck dumb. The revolution of time and its decisions have defeated reason and knowledge.

—A survivor of a Mongol invasion

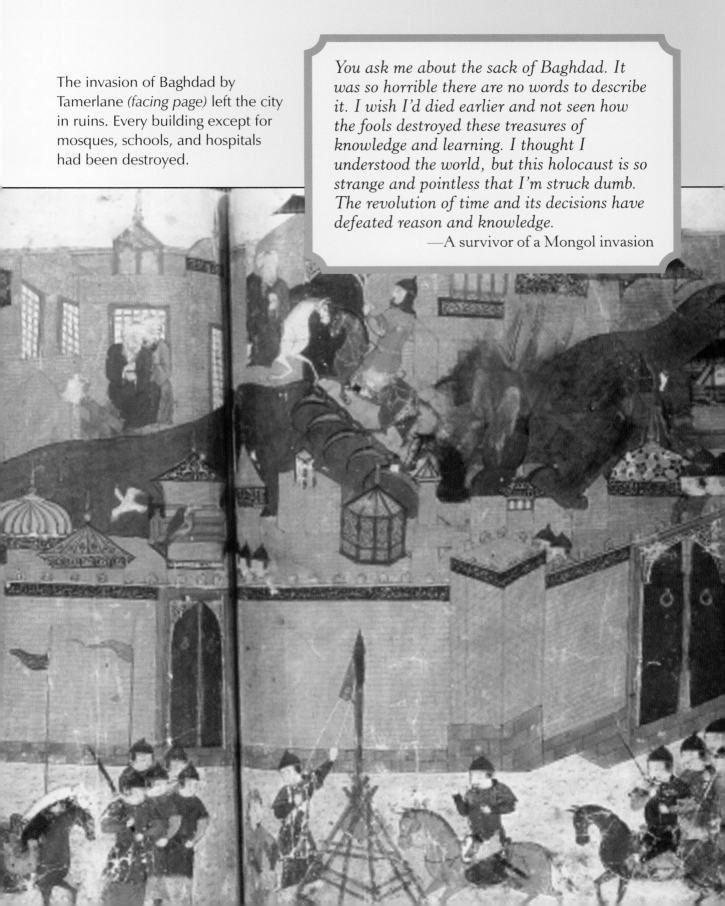

The Family Jewels

The women of Baghdad wore jewelry to be fashionable and to display the family's wealth. Few people trusted local banks or currency. When they sold goods or services, they converted the money into necklaces, bracelets, and other jewelry made from gold and gems. Women wore the jewelry for safekeeping. When money was needed, the family sold a set of earrings or a pendant for cash. Men did not wear jewelry, but they carried gold or jeweled knives, guns, or swords on special occasions.

Clothing in Baghdad

A hot, usually sunny city, Baghdad was surrounded by deserts. During the summer, the temperature often exceeded 100 degrees. People wore loose clothing and head coverings that offered protection from the heat and the sun. They wore sandals or shoes with pointy toes.

Women put on a veil and an *abayah*—a loose, black cloak that covered them from head to foot. Women used cosmetics and perfumes and lined their eyes with black kohl. They used henna (a reddish brown dye) to color their nails and to paint decorative designs on their fingers and hands. They arranged their hair in waves, curls, braids, and ringlets, and they wore anklets and bracelets. Women's elaborate, dome-shaped headdresses were decorated with jewels or gold coins. Young girls went in loose dresses until they reached puberty, when most began to wear a veil and other adult clothes.

Men wore an ankle-length robe called a caftan, along with a turban or a *cheffiyeh*—a head cloth held in place with a cord known as an *agal*. Young boys wore loose shirts and pants, sometimes accompanied by a skullcap. These clothing styles remained the traditional dress of Baghdad for hundreds of years.

The loose clothing styles of medieval Baghdad *(left and opposite page)* allowed cooling air to move freely about the body.

The Ottoman Takeover

Baghdad's location became a disadvantage when the Islamic Empire was destroyed. Every empire in the Middle East wanted to control the fertile land between the Tigris and the Euphrates.

In 1534 a Turkish sultan (ruler), Süleyman the Magnificent, captured the city. In 1624 Shah Abbas I of Persia took Baghdad. He leveled its buildings and massacred members of the Sunni sect. In 1638 Baghdad was recaptured by Sultan Murad IV and incorporated as a province of the vast Ottoman Empire.

The Ottoman sultans worked hard to hold on to Baghdad. They ruled Baghdad through a local government that tried to control the city's many independent factions and ethnic groups. The sultans taxed people heavily. Tenants had to pay their landlords large sums, which were handed over to the empire. But the taxes weren't invested in the city's industry or used to keep the ancient irrigation system functioning. Instead the Ottoman rulers used the money in other parts of their large empire. Starvation and disease became rampant in Baghdad. The population shrank as some people left the city to begin new lives as nomads.

In the early nineteenth century, the Ottoman sultan Mahmud II worked for the allegiance of Baghdad's people. He imported teachers and technology from Europe and founded schools that taught European customs.

Mahmud believed that by changing the way people dressed, he could change their attitudes and way of life. He banned traditional Arab clothing, including long robes, turbans, and headgear. Baghdad's male residents were forced to wear coats and Turkish fezzes—flat-topped, round hats with tassels.

In 1831 an outbreak of bubonic plague devastated the population of Baghdad. Thousands of people died, and unburied corpses littered the streets. Later that year, the Tigris swelled over its banks to cause one of the worst floods in Baghdad's history. More than 7,000 homes were wiped out on the first day. The two disasters killed two-thirds of the city's population.

The Turkish sultan Süleyman the Magnificent *(seated, opposite)* took the throne in 1520, beginning his famous reign over the Ottoman Empire.

Nomadic Life

The Ottoman Empire struggled to control its many territories, including Baghdad. As the nineteenth century progressed, the empire's grasp weakened. The authority of family groups became more important in Baghdad than the empire's rule. As Baghdad declined, some of the city's residents left their urban dwellings for village life. In turn, some of the villagers left their rural homes to travel with groups of Bedouin, or desert nomads.

Nomads had played a role in Baghdad's life and economy since the city's founding. Indeed, the boundary between village life and the nomads' territory fluctuated constantly with changes in weather, irrigation, and political rule. A year of good weather and relative peace meant that a village on the city's outskirts would be able to grow a successful crop. The next year, if it did not rain enough or if damaged canals were not repaired because of political fighting, the villagers'

Nomads' lives revolved around the seasons, which dictated the direction of their travels.

crops might shrivel up and die. In response, villagers might forsake their farms and become nomads.

Some nomads raised sheep and goats at the edge of Baghdad's farming villages. Others raised camels and wandered in search of pasture. The nomads relied on camels for transportation, food, and milk. They used camel hides to make tents, clothing, and water flasks, and they harvested camel dung for fuel. During the summer, camel herders camped in camel-hair tents near villages. During the winter and spring, when Baghdad traditionally experiences 90 percent of its annual rainfall, the herders wandered deeper into the desert to graze their camels.

Nomads knew that a family's possessions could be wiped out by an enemy raid or a drought. Many nomads valued displays of courage and wisdom. A chief was expected to treat all male members of the band as equals and to make decisions that were right for everyone. Nomadic women were less likely to wear a veil than urban women. But as in the cities, women were supposed to be subservient to their fathers, husbands, and brothers.

May your table always be spread.
—Saying to be spoken by a guest
to the host after a meal

Hospitality

Demonstrating hospitality to friends and strangers alike is important to the Muslim code of honor. For a Muslim to refuse another's hospitality would be to disgrace himself; for a guest to refuse a Muslim's hospitality would be to greatly offend the host. Simply asking for directions might lead to an invitation into the stranger's house for coffee and baklava (a sweet pastry).

Hospitality to friends and strangers was so important that most homes on Baghdad's outskirts were equipped with special guest houses or tents. Even enemies traveling in small groups of four or five were welcomed as guests. In the harsh desert environment, a host never knew when he himself might be in need of hospitality.

Guests typically stopped at the first tent they came to and were immediately invited in. The women of the house might seat the guests on a handmade carpet and begin to prepare a meal. If a cold night had fallen, the guests would be allowed to warm themselves by the fire. While dinner cooked, women might serve salt and biscuits, pomegranates, or sugar soaked in rose water. Visitors drank tiny cupfuls of very strong coffee that was heavily spiced with cardamom.

Hosts served guests the best in the house. This could mean a feast. Chickens, sheep, and sometimes even camels were butchered. Meat was served in stews or atop deep beds of rice spread on large platters. Guests would show their enjoyment of a meal by eating slowly, a sign of politeness and a custom believed to promote good health.

45

The Magic of Baghdad's Carpets

When the Ottoman Empire conquered Baghdad, it absorbed the city's cultural and natural resources. One valuable trade was Baghdad's rich history of carpet making. Baghdad's artisans adopted the art from the Persians, who had learned the skill from the Egyptians. Persian workers used their skill in design and color to develop a unique style, which they passed on to the people of Baghdad.

Some families, especially those living in Baghdad's more rural areas, set up looms in their homes. Many carpets were produced in city workshops, where men and women wove them on large looms. *Asalim*, or foremen, called out the sequence of colors so that weavers could create uniform designs. Patterns remained traditionally Persian in design. Some illustrated the garden paradise Muslims believed awaited them after death. Others featured geometric patterns all facing in the same direction. The carpets could then be pointed toward Mecca during prayers.

Not only did carpets offer an important source of income, they were an important household item. Travelers or members of a caravan never left home without enough carpets to line the tents where they slept at night. Carpets were fashioned into saddle bags that were strapped to the backs of camels, horses, and donkeys. Prayer rugs were just large enough for one person to kneel on. A Muslim in prayer would point the rug in the direction of Mecca, then kneel and touch the forehead to the far end of the rug.

Carpets proved to be a valuable commodity for Baghdad. In the fifteenth century, European countries such as Portugal, England, and Poland became interested in trading their goods for carpets made in the Middle East. Over the centuries, beautiful carpets found their way into palaces and ordinary homes across Europe and the United States.

Baghdad's finest carpets were woven from silk. To determine a carpet's value, a merchant laid his thumb on the carpet's edge and counted the threads within the breadth of his thumb. The more threads, the greater the carpet's value.

Baghdad under Midhat

In the late 1860s, the sultan who ruled the Ottoman Empire appointed a new governor named Midhat to rule Baghdad.

Midhat made many reforms that improved the lives of Baghdad's people. He ordered the city's debris-filled canals to be cleaned and reopened. Farmers whose land had been dried out or flooded as the canal system disintegrated were once again able to grow food. Midhat established land reform laws that enabled people to purchase property. This encouraged nomadic leaders to opt for a more settled existence. Many exchanged their camel-hair tents for brick houses and replaced their dependence on the camel with a new reliance on commercial trade. Some became powerful landowners.

The balance of power shifted from family authority to urban government. Midhat reorganized the government to give

When Midhat (seated, inset) was appointed to govern Baghdad, one of his first tasks was to rebuild the city. Baghdad was showing alarming signs of decay— including this mosque along the Tigris (right)—after centuries of war, fire, and floods.

people more representation and developed a system of criminal and commercial law. He founded schools, creating a secular (nonreligious) school system that expanded the existing Islam-based system. European languages began to be taught.

Modernization soon arrived in Baghdad. In 1836 Baghdad saw its first steamboats and in 1861 its first telegraph. As a result, Baghdad's commercial trade improved. Landowners began to export cash crops. Imported goods began flowing into the city in 1869, when the Suez Canal linked the Mediterranean and the Red Seas.

Under the leadership of this Turkish governor, Baghdad began to move from having a subsistence economy toward being part of an international marketplace. These major economic changes began to raise the standard of living for Baghdad's people and to change its social and cultural norms as well. Social status had been traditionally linked to one's noble lineage, fighting prowess, and religious training. A good education and property ownership became new ways for people to climb the social ladder and to acquire wealth.

Independence

At the dawn of the twentieth century, crude oil (petroleum) was discovered in the Middle East. The invention of oil-fueled ships, airplanes, and cars made petroleum one of the most valuable substances on earth—and reason to go to war. In World War I (1914–1918), the Ottoman Empire sided with the Central Powers (Germany and the Austro-Hungarian Empire) against the Allies (Britain, France, Russia, the United States, and several other nations). In 1917 the British captured Baghdad, promising to return the city to independence from foreign influence.

World War I ended with the defeat of the Central Powers. The British established the constitutional monarchy of Iraq. In 1921 the British crowned King Faisal I *(right)* ruler of Iraq, basing the monarchy in Baghdad. A decade later, the British withdrew, and Iraq became an independent nation. Foreign-owned oil companies based in the city brought new jobs to Baghdad. But most of the money the companies earned left Iraq. Rich landowners held Iraq's wealth and power. By 1958 the decades of change had begun to unravel Baghdad's traditional society. A middle class—neither rich nor poor—was emerging.

On July 14, 1958, the army rose up under General Abdul Karim Kassam to abolish Iraq's monarchy. King Faisal II and the prime minister were killed. A republic—a government composed of elected officials—was founded in place of the monarchy. Baghdad's residents poured into the streets to support the revolution. But the revolution woke sleeping conflicts between certain families, among different ethnic groups, and between the Sunni and Shia sects of Islam.

Images of Iraq's president, Saddam Hussein, are easy to find in Baghdad's public places.

Food in Baghdad

Food is a central part of Baghdad's social life. In a family home, the scene may be similar to what it was in the city's early days. If guests are present, men may sit in a separate room from the women. Food is served on large trays set on the floor or low tables. Diners sit on cushions on the floor and, as custom dictates, use only their right hand to eat from common dishes. Eating without utensils is a sign to a host that the guest is enjoying the food.

Servants or the women of the house prepare meals for guests. Various appetizers, soups, salads, main dishes, and desserts are served. Unleavened (flat) bread called *samoon* and a yogurt drink called *laban* are served at every meal. Other popular dishes include boiled lamb with rice and kabobs—pieces of lamb and tomato roasted on skewers over an open fire. Fishers sometimes land a Tigris River fish known as *masgouf,* which they grill right on the riverbank. At important

A Baghdad family (far left) gathers to share a meal. In the markets, coffee vendors (left) brew pots of thick, spiced coffee to sell by the cup.

dinner parties, hosts may serve an entire sheep stuffed with rice, almonds, pine nuts, peppers, tomatoes, eggplant, cabbage, and spices.

Baghdad is famous for its sweet desserts, such as baklava or cream-filled pastries covered in mountains of fruit. Another favorite dessert is *ma'mounia*, a kind of pudding first made for a ninth-century caliph who requested a dessert worthy of a king. Coffee is the city's most popular beverage.

Ma'mounia

You will need:
- 3 cups of water
- 2 cups of sugar
- 1 tsp. lemon juice
- ½ cup unsalted butter
- 1 cup semolina (hard-wheat flour)
- 1 tsp. ground cinnamon

Dissolve sugar in water over low heat. Add lemon juice and bring to boil. Let mixture simmer about 10 minutes until syrupy. In another pan, melt butter, then add semolina and stir until lightly browned. Add syrup and stir constantly. Simmer 10 minutes, then let cool for 20 minutes. Spoon into bowls; top with whipped cream and cinnamon.

Changing Times

The revolution of 1958 radically changed Baghdad society. The landowners lost some power to the urban workers, peasants, and members of the middle class. More people aspired to professions such as law, politics, administration, and education.

The influx of new technology, fashion, and consumption habits began to change Baghdad's traditional way of life. Long-established artisans were forced to compete with retailers who sold inexpensive, mass-produced imitations of local goods. Potters, tailors, shoemakers, blacksmiths, and other artisans had to seek new work. Some became sellers of products rather than producers. By the 1970s, oil revenues had improved living conditions for many in Baghdad. More people had the chance to go to school and to receive modern medical care.

In 1979 Iraq's president, Saddam Hussein al-Takrit came to power. Within days of assuming the presidency, the new leader had killed 500 politicians and military leaders he suspected as enemies.

In 1980 religious differences led to war between Iraq and its neighbor Iran. The long, devastating war went on for eight years with thousands of casualties. On August 2, 1990, two years after that war ended, Iraq invaded neighboring Kuwait, an independent nation that Iraq had claimed when a monarchy. Four days later, the United Nations imposed harsh economic sanctions, forbidding Iraq from exporting its oil or engaging in trade with other nations, except for medicine and food. In January 1991, a coalition including Britain, France, the United States, Egypt, and Saudi Arabia launched a massive air and land war against Iraq.

The war, Operation Desert Storm, ended on April 6, 1991, when Iraq accepted a UN cease-fire agreement. An estimated 100,000 Iraqi soldiers had died, and several hundred thousand were wounded. Some 150,000 Iraqi soldiers deserted. Coalition forces had 343 casualties.

Experts estimate that at least 15,000 Iraqi civilians died as a direct result of coalition bombings, which leveled much of Baghdad. That, along with continued economic sanctions, led to epidemics of disease and starvation among Baghdad's people. Damage to water systems made the city an unhealthy place to live.

In 1995 the UN began allowing Iraq to sell some of its oil in exchange for food and medicine. Although the easing of oil-export limits has helped, Iraq's economic problems are so extensive that many families still do not have access to adequate food and medicine.

Before the Iran-Iraq War, students flocked to schools of higher learning such as Saddam Hussein University in Baghdad (*left*). But years of war leveled many buildings and disrupted daily life (*below*).

A Modern City

For the most part, Baghdad is a modern city. Many men and women wear pants and shirts, although others choose to wear the culture's traditional dress. Families continue to be an important nucleus of Baghdad's culture. Baghdad's men and women continue to observe a tradition of gender segregation, although it is not as strict as it once was. They often socialize separately, and it is common for most homes to include separate living rooms for men and women. Men dominate family and societal life. But women's rights have advanced greatly. Many women work outside the home.

In 1978 the government passed an amendment to a law that called for the emancipation (freeing) of women on a number of levels. Women were given more rights in matters of marriage, divorce, and child custody. They were given greater access to education and made advances in the workplace. During the Iran-Iraq War in the 1980s, many men served in the military, and more women took jobs. These days women can go to college. Many hold professional positions such as lawyers, doctors, engineers, teachers, and welfare workers. Adult women are allowed to vote and be elected to public office. But many people abide by ancient customs.

Most marriages in modern-day Baghdad are arranged by the family of the bride and groom, just as in the days of the caliphs. Before the wedding, the groom pays a dowry to the father of the bride. Weddings are celebrated with great pomp and extravagance.

Funerals also remain occasions central to the culture of Baghdad. Female relatives stay indoors for 40 days and dress only in black for the year-long mourning period. Bodies of the dead are perfumed with special oils and covered with a shroud. In Muslim funerals, bodies are buried so that the face points toward the holy city of Mecca.

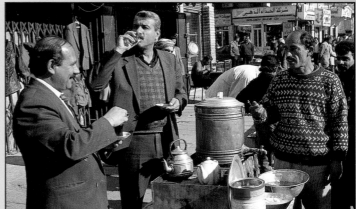

Scenes from Baghdad: Schoolchildren volunteer answers in class *(top)*, women in traditional clothes browse along a street of wedding shops *(left),* and men gather for a cup of streetside coffee *(above).*

Traditional silhouettes tower above the buzz of modern traffic *(above)*. Elsewhere in Baghdad, new state-sponsored housing goes up *(right)*. On Fridays the city shuts down as the faithful are called to prayer *(facing page)*.

Baghdad, Old and New

Modern Baghdad, home to more than three million people, is an interesting mix of old and new. A poor economy in the 1950s caused many people to migrate from rural areas to the city. Many of the city's residents live in mud-brick homes, although Iraq's government has been working to accommodate Baghdad's growing population with better housing. Well-off city dwellers live in brick apartments or houses with swimming pools and palm trees.

The city's modern district of Karkh on the west bank of the Tigris contains banks, hotels, high-rise buildings, and elegant avenues. The old section of the city, called Rusefeh, retains the narrow streets and open-air suqs reminiscent of ancient Baghdad. Baghdad houses the nation's government and principal industries along with an airport and several universities.

Islam still dominates the lives of Baghdad's people. Although the ancient union between religion and state has been weakened, Islam continues to be the official state religion and influences everything from education and marriage laws to business and banking practices. On Friday, the Muslim holy day, many of Baghdad's stores and businesses close.

Muslims gather at noon to worship in mosques and to give alms to the poor. Schools still emphasize the study of the Koran and the system of rote learning and memorization. They also teach modern math, science, and foreign languages.

Despite Iraq's economic problems, Baghdad's marketplaces bustle with activity. Merchants sell hand-woven carpets, jewelry made of gold and silver, and sweet-smelling coffee, tea, and spices. Baghdad boasts eight remarkable museums. Beautifully crafted palaces, mosques, parks, restaurants, and cafés present a colorful and lively example of a modern society with ancient roots.

Baghdad Timeline

3000 B.C. to A.D. 762
Early History

3000 B.C.	Sumer invents writing system in Mesopotamia
1900 B.C.	Babylonians establish their capital of Babylon in Mesopotamia
1350 B.C.	The Assyrians overrun Mesopotamia and establish their capital of Nineveh

A.D. 610	The prophet Muhammad has first spiritual revelation
A.D. 630	The Muslims conquer Mecca, and it becomes spiritual center of Islam
A.D. 634	The Islamic Empire occupies Iraq, a territory held by the Persians
A.D. 640	The Islamic Empire conquers Persian Empire
A.D. 747	The Abbasid dynasty assumes control of Islamic Empire
A.D. 751	Islamic forces defeat Chinese army and discover craft of papermaking
A.D. 756	Spain breaks away from Islamic Empire

A.D. 762–1258
The Abbasid Caliphate

A.D. 762	The Abbasid caliph al-Mansur founds Baghdad as his new capital
A.D. 786	Harun al-Rashid becomes the caliph of Baghdad
A.D. 788	Morocco breaks away from Islamic Empire
A.D. 794	Baghdad builds its first paper mill
A.D. 800	Tunisia breaks away from Islamic Empire
A.D. 809	Caliph Harun al-Rashid dies, and war erupts between his two sons
A.D. 813	Harun's son al-Ma'mun defeats his brother and becomes caliph
A.D. 825	Caliph al-Ma'mun marries Buran in an extravagant wedding
A.D. 833	Caliph al-Mustasim installs Baghdad's first Mamluk army
A.D. 850	Caliph al-Mutawakkil restricts rights of Baghdad's dhimmis, or non-Muslims
A.D. 868	Egypt breaks away from Islamic Empire
A.D. 1146	Palace of Caliph al-Muqtafi catches fire

A.D. 1258–1932 The Occupations	**A.D. 1258**	The Mongol Hülegü Khan conquers Baghdad, ending Abbasid rule
	A.D. 1401	The Mongol ruler Tamerlane sacks Baghdad
	A.D. 1534	The Turkish sultan Süleyman the Magnificent conquers Baghdad
	A.D. 1624	The Persian shah Abbas takes Baghdad and slaughters Sunni inhabitants
	A.D. 1638	The Turkish sultan Murad IV recaptures Baghdad
	A.D. 1704	*One Thousand and One Nights* is translated into English and becomes an immediate success
	A.D. 1831	Baghdad's population is decimated by an outbreak of bubonic plague and flooding of the Tigris River
	A.D. 1869	Reform-minded governor Midhat takes over; Suez Canal opens
	A.D. 1900	Oil is discovered in the Middle East around the turn of the century
	A.D. 1917	The British occupy Baghdad
	A.D. 1921	King Faisal I is crowned ruler of Iraq
	A.D. 1924	Iraq and Britain sign treaty of alliance
	A.D. 1932	Iraq becomes a sovereign state
A.D. 1932– Independence	**A.D. 1945**	Iraq founds the Arab League
	A.D. 1958	Revolution abolishes the monarchy in bloody coup d'état; King Faisal II killed; Iraq declared a republic
	A.D. 1968	The Baath political party takes control of the Iraqi government
	A.D. 1979	Saddam Hussein becomes president of Iraq
	A.D. 1980	Iraq goes to war with Iran
	A.D. 1988	The Iran-Iraq War ends in a cease-fire
	A.D. 1990	Iran invades Kuwait
	A.D. 1991	Iraq is defeated in the Persian Gulf War
	A.D. 1999	Baghdad's population reaches 6 million

Books about Iraq and Baghdad

Bratman Fred. *War in the Persian Gulf*. Brookfield, Connecticut: The Millbrook Press, 1991.

Docherty, J. P. *Iraq*. New York: Chelsea House Publishers, 1988.

Hassig, Susan M. *Iraq*. North Bellmore, New York: Marshall Cavendish, 1993.

Iraq in Pictures. Minneapolis: Lerner Publications Company, 1990.

Kent, Zachary. *The Persian Gulf War*. Springfield, New Jersey: Enslow Publishers, Inc., 1994.

Kramer, Samuel Noah. *Cradle of Civilization*. New York: Time, Inc., 1967.

Merrell Foster, Leila. *Iraq: Enchantment of the World*. Chicago: Children's Press, 1991.

Nardo, Don. *The Persian Gulf War*. San Diego: Lucent Books, 1991.

Pierce, Joe E. *Understanding the Middle East*. Rutland, Vermont: Charles E. Tuttle Co., 1971.

Ratzesberger, Anna. *Camel Bells: A Boy of Baghdad*. Chicago: Albert Whitman, 1935.

Spencer, Dr. William. *The Middle East*. Guilford, Connecticut: The Dushkin Publishing Group, Inc., 1994.

Stewart, Desmond. *Early Islam*. New York: Time Life, 1967.

Index

About the Author and Illustrator

Dawn Kotapish is a writer and editor living in Oak Park, Illinois. She has traveled widely throughout the Middle East and lived for a number of years in a region of Saudi Arabia just south of Iraq. She has worked as an English teacher in Chicago, West Africa, and Nepal. This is her first children's book.

Ray Webb of Woodstock, England, studied art and design at Birmingham Polytechnic in Birmingham, England. A specialist in historical and scientific subjects, his work has been published in Britain, the Netherlands, Germany, and the United States. He continues to teach and lecture and especially enjoys introducing young people to illustration as a career opportunity.

Acknowledgments

For quoted material: p. 7, 14, 28, Hitti, Philip K. *Capital Cities of Arab Islam.* (Minneapolis: University of Minnesota Press, 1973); p. 10, 23, Gurthrie, Shirley. *Arab Social Life in the Middle Ages.* (London: Saqi Books, 1995); p. 12, Levy, Reuben. *A Baghdad Chronicle.* (Cambridge University Press, 1929); p. 26, Wiet, Gaston. *Baghdad: Metropolis of the Abbasid Caliphate.* (University of Oklahoma Press, 1971); p. 30, Hitti, Philip K. *The Arabs.* (South Bend, Indiana: Princeton University, Regnery/Gateway Inc., 1943); p. 37, *Legacy—Iraq: The Cradle of Civilization.* (Ambrose Video Publishing, Inc.)

For photographs and art reproductions: Louvre, Paris/Bridgeman Art Library, London/New York, p. 6; Stock Montage, p. 7; Special Collections, Smathers Library, University of Florida, Gainseville, p. 11; Christie's Images/ SuperStock/North Wind Pictures, pp. 12–13; Bibliotheque National de France, pp. 22–23; The Granger Collection, New York, pp. 31, 32–33, 34, 41; The Granger Collection, New York/Bridgeman Art Library, London/ New York, p. 36 (inset); Bibliotheque National de France/Bridgeman Art Library, London/New York, pp. 36–37; Mary Evans Picture Library, London, pp. 38–39; Christie's Images/ SuperStock, pp. 42–43; Archive Photos/ Stock Montage, pp. 48 (inset), 48–49; Liaison International, Middle East Centre, St. Anthony's College, Oxford, pp. 50–51; Liaison International, pp. 52–53, 54–55; Jockel Finck, AP-Wide World, pp. 56–57; Caroline Penn/Panos Pictures, pp. 57, 58–59. Cover: Christie's Images/SuperStock/North Wind Pictures.